THE BOOK OF

MOVEMENT EXPLORATION

Can You Move Like This?

Also by John M. Feierabend, published by GIA Publications, Inc.:
The Book of Echo Songs
The Book of Call and Response
The Book of Fingerplays and Action Songs
The Book of Children's SongTales
The Book of Beginning Circle Games
The Book of Songs and Rhymes with Beat Motions
The Book of Pitch Exploration

For infants and toddlers:
The Book of Lullabies
The Book of Wiggles and Tickles
The Book of Simple Songs and Circles
The Book of Bounces
The Book of Tapping and Clapping

On compact disc for infants and toddlers:
'Round and 'Round the Garden: Music in My First Year!
Ride Away on Your Horses: Music, Now I'm One!
Frog in the Meadow: Music, Now I'm Two!

On DVD and Compact Disc by Peggy Lyman and John M. Feierabend:
Move It! Expressive Movements with Classical Music

G-5876

THE BOOK OF
MOVEMENT EXPLORATION

Can You Move Like This?

John M. Feierabend & Jane Kahan

GIA PUBLICATIONS, INC. • CHICAGO

Compiled by
John M. Feierabend
First Steps in Music, LLC

www.giamusic.com/feierabend

Copyright © 2003
GIA Publications, Inc.
7404 S. Mason Avenue
Chicago, IL 60638

Printed in the
United States of America.
ISBN 1-57999-264-1

Table of Contents

Introduction

hich one of us has not enjoyed "dancing around the living room"? These are wonderful moments of uninhibited response to music or mood.

This book contains a rich collection of activities that present many possibilities for movement for children. Through engaging in these activities, children will develop a movement vocabulary as they develop their gross motor skills and enhance their creative movement ideas.

These Movement Exploration activities will bring out the strong movement impulses as well as the gentle ones. Some activities explore fast or slow, sudden or sustained, heavy or light movements. Other activities explore the possibilities of moving in response to a partner or a group of other children.

Children can enjoy these activities silently or with accompanying music, building an appreciation for moving with music as well as being moved by music.

These Movement Explorations are delightful to experience in themselves, but they can also lead to more proficient skills when engaged in other more structured movement activities such as Finger Plays, Action Songs, Circle Games and dances.

Enjoy these activities as you discover your movement potential!

John M. Feierabend & Jane Kahan

Jane Kahan *teaches dance at Dayton's Bluff Elementary School in St. Paul and is an expert on the movement theories of Rudolph Laban.* John M. Feierabend *is a professor and chair of the music education division at The Hartt School of the University of Hartford in Connecticut.*

Foreword

Have you ever enjoyed reacting to music by "dancing around the living room"? If you have, you know what a wonderful experience it is to "be one with the music," communicating through movement with the expressive artistry of the composer. The depth of ability to express ourselves through movement, however, depends upon the development of our personal movement vocabulary. Movement exploration activities enrich us in two ways. They help us become aware of the various ways our body can move alone and with others and, when accompanied by music, they help us stylistically connect with the expressive intent of the composer. What better way to discover how music can move you than to move with music!

This book organizes movement exploration activities according to ten movement themes that are inspired by the work of Rudolf von Laban, a Hungarian-born dancer who studied human movement and inspired several generations of dancers and educators. He analyzed human movement qualities, created a system of dance notation, and taught many important dancers and dance educators.

Within the ten themes, activities are presented with and without suggested accompanying music and should be thought of as recipes in a cookbook. No one would want to prepare meals consistently from only one section in

the cookbook. Activities should be selected from the various themes to provide a balanced movement/dance diet for the child.

A movement/dance teacher might create an entire movement lesson by selecting an activity or two from several themes. A music teacher would more likely select one or two activities from one theme as a part of a single music lesson. During subsequent lessons however, other activities from other themes should then be explored. As children become more experienced with different combinations of movement and sample a variety of themes, their own movement/dance ideas can emerge and become more varied.

Some movement activities are offered throughout the book as a sample of how movement explorations can be combined with music to enhance the movement activity as well as develop sensitivities to the expressive qualities of the music.

Some of these activities are simple enough for nursery and preschool children; others are more suited to children in the early elementary grades. The amount of experience the children have will also determine the level of difficulty. Select those activities that are best suited to the abilities of the children you teach.

It is a good idea for children to see sample movement possibilities as well as hear about them. Therefore, chil-dren benefit by having the teacher or an experienced student dance for the class to model how certain movements might look. In addition, the teacher should occasionally video-tape, for the children to see, short segments of the children performing movement activities.

It is our hope that the activities presented in this book will serve as a starting point and you too will be inspired to create, along with your students, wonder-full movement/dance experiences.

Following is a checklist of the 10 Movement Themes. Use it as a guide to keep track of which themes have been explored and which ones should be explored in the future. When all the themes have been explored, begin the checklist over again with new activities.

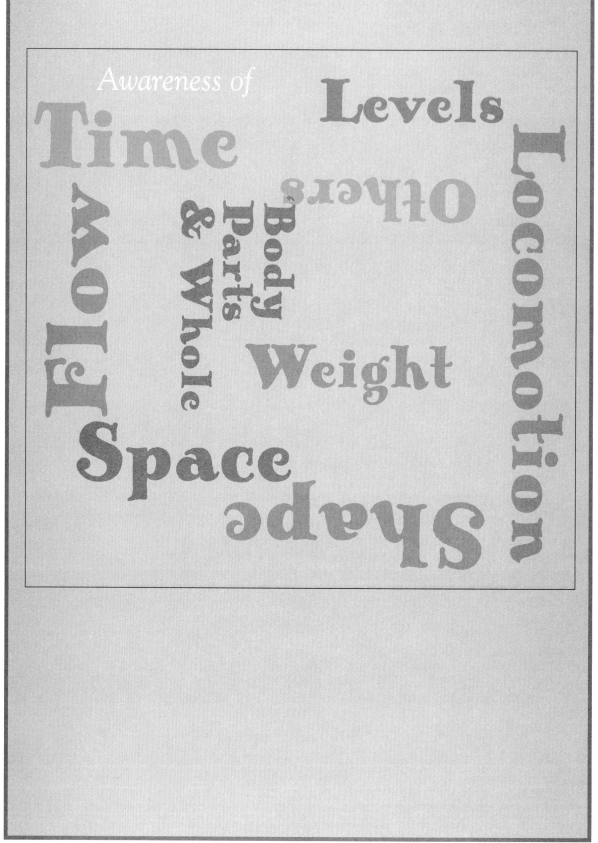

Awareness of

Time

Levels

Locomotion

Flow

Others

Body Parts & Whole

Weight

Space

Shape

Movement Themes Checklist *(Adapted from Rudolf von Laban)*

Feel free to photo copy this page for your use.

1. Awareness of Body Parts and Whole

- [ ] 1.1 Whole Body Movement
- [ ] 1.2 Isolated Body Parts
- [ ] 1.3 Leading With a Part
- [ ] 1.4 Initiating With a Part

2. Awareness of Time

- [ ] 2.1 Quick and Slow Movement
- [ ] 2.2 Clock Time

3. Awareness of Space

- [ ] 3.1 Personal Space and General Space
- [ ] 3.2 Direct/Indirect Pathway (Straight/Twisted)
- [ ] 3.3 Inward Movement (Narrow)
- [ ] 3.4 Outward Movement (Wide)
- [ ] 3.5 Direction of Movement
- [ ] 3.6 Distance of Movement

4. Awareness of Levels

- [ ] 4.1 High/Middle/Low

5. Awareness of Weight

- [ ] 5.1 Heavy/Light
- [ ] 5.2 Strong/Gentle
- [ ] 5.3 Tense/Relaxed

6. Awareness of Locomotion

- [ ] *(walking, leaping, running, hopping, jumping, skipping, galloping, striding, sliding, crawling, rolling, tiptoe, stomping, etc.)*

7. Awareness of Flow

- [ ] 7.1 Sudden/Sustained
- [ ] 7.2 Sequential/Simultaneous
- [ ] 7.3 Bound/Free

8. Awareness of Shape

- [ ] 8.1 Becoming Shapes

9. Awareness of Others

- [ ] 9.1 Partners
- [ ] 9.2 Groups

10. Student Created Movement

- [ ] 10.1 Representative Movement
- [ ] 10.2 Non-Representative Movement

Theme 10 should be sampled and returned to after every few lessons. It is during Theme 10 that students are most free to create movement in response to music. As they acquire more movement experiences, their creative efforts will become more and more interesting.

The Five-Course Meal for Movement Classes

When classes can be entirely constructed of movement experiences, a five-course "soup to nuts" menu should be offered. When movement exploration activities can only be part of a larger lesson, as is often the case in music classes, the teacher should rotate through the menu. The full menu would include:

The First Course - Games

Begin the class with a game; an activity that is playful and gets the children's attention. The rules of the game should focus attention on a movement concept that will be further explored later in the lesson. This first game is also a good way to include reluctant explorers. Play a game of "Freeze Tag." Children walk around (or run) trying to avoid being tagged and must freeze if they are tagged. They stay frozen until someone comes near and copies their shape. Extensions: If working on levels have them stay frozen until someone comes over and makes a shape at a different level. If working on letter shapes, then stay frozen until someone comes over and copies the letter or names it or makes a different letter.

The Second Course - Warm Up

These experiences help develop children's bodies for strenuous activity. Children often appear to be instantly ready for strenuous activity; however, some time should be spent teaching a few traditional dance stretches. During these activities it is worthwhile to explore how our bodies feel different from day to day.

The Third Course - Across the Floor

This is a traditional activity in most dance classes. Visit a ballet, modern, jazz, African or tap class for any age or skill level and you will see students traveling across the space in rows. Children benefit from working in small groups of two or three, while others watch and learn while waiting their turn. This is also an excellent time for teachers to assess the children's movement development and learn from their responses.

The Fourth Course - Improvisation

This is the main course. Tasks are assigned which allow the children to concurrently explore their own solutions. Children are free to experiment, explore, discover and invent movement of their own to meet the task. These activities are more anonymous than the Across the Floor or Composition activities because all children are working and no one is watching.

The Fifth Course - Composition/Ending Activities

These activities give a feeling of completion. Just as some meals end with an elaborate dessert, some end with fruit and some end with just coffee, a class can be brought to completion in a variety of ways. A composition assignment could be used so that each student performs one final time. Or perhaps a movement sequence could be used to serve as a ritual good-bye. A composition requires students to create a series of movements that become a set that can then be repeated the same way more than once.

Theme 1

Awareness of BODY PARTS & WHOLE

Theme 1: Awareness of Body Parts & Whole

1.1 Whole Body Movement

Are You Moving or Not?

Have the students touch the floor. "Is the floor moving?" Tell them to stand and be "as still as the floor." Tell them whenever you say, "freeze" they should be as still as the floor.

Stop and Go Dance

Teacher chants, "Go, go, go, go, freeze." Students are encouraged to move around the room in different ways, such as run, twirl, wiggle, etc…

The End Is Near

Have students practice moving and stopping as you chant, "I think I hear the ending coming and now it's time to STOP."

Listen and Move

Use an instrument such as a hand drum or wood sticks. Tell the students to move around the room when they hear the instrument and stop when the instrument stops. Divide the class in half and tell half to move when they hear the instrument and stop when there is silence and tell the other half to move when there is silence and stop when they hear the instrument.

Paper Plate Balancing

Give each student a paper plate. Tell them to choose a part of their body to balance the plate on. Have the students move around the room. If the plate falls they must freeze until someone comes along and hands them their plate. The person picking up the plate must continue to balance his/her plate also. Once the plate has been returned they should select a new place to balance the plate.

Shake and Freeze

Tell the students to shake their bodies as you shake a tambourine and chant the words, "Shake, shake, shake, shake, shake, shake, FREEZE!" Repeat and ask them to shake something else. Repeat several times asking them to shake something else. Ask them to see how many things they can shake at the same time. Relax. (This also explores 1.2 Isolated Body Parts.)

Whirl and Stop

Tell the students to whirl around while you chant, "Whirl and whirl and whirl and STOP!" Repeat and ask students to whirl another part of their body. Repeat several times asking them to whirl something new. Ask how many parts can whirl at the same time. Relax. (This also explores 1.2 Isolated Body Parts.)

See also: 4.1 Counting Shapes

1.2 Isolated Body Parts

Put It Somewhere

Tell the students to dance with their thumbs while you play on a drum. When the drum stops they should put their thumb on the floor. Repeat dancing with different body parts (Head, elbow, etc…). Each time the drum stops place body parts somewhere (wall, on someone else, etc…).

Read My Mind

Before beginning, think of a body part. Tell the students you are thinking of a body part and they should start moving some body part to guess which one it is. If no one is moving the body part say, "I don't see anyone moving it." When one or more are moving the correct body part say, "I see 3 people moving it." "I see 5 people moving it." Students should look around and try each other's motions until more and more are doing the same motion. "Almost everyone's doing it." Finally the teacher will be able to say, "I see everyone moving it."

John's Knee

Have the students stand in small circles of 8-10. The first person says their name and names a body part while moving that body part, such as "John's knee." (John would lift and lower his knee while saying this.) All in the circle repeat "John's knee" and perform the same motion. The next student says his/her name and a different body part, such as "Jane's elbow." All repeat, "Jane's elbow" (with the appropriate motion) followed by "John's knee" (with the appropriate motion). Continue with each student until all in the circle are saying all the names and performing all the different motions creating a movement phrase. Trying performing the movement phrase faster or silently.

Variations: Have the students stand in one large circle but only perform the last three motions with their own. Or after the names and motions are learned, have the students scatter around the room and perform the entire movement phrase.

The Most Important Part

Tell students this dance will feature a part of their body. They should dance with their whole body but draw special attention to one part in many ways. For example, if the most important part was a hand you could shake it, swing it, raise it, clap it, or tap it on the floor. Ask students to come up with other possible ways to draw attention to that body part. The teacher should accompany this activity with a percussion instrument. When the students hear the rhythm they should move and stop when the rhythm stops. When the rhythm begins again they should begin featuring a new important part of their body.

Duet for Two Body Parts

Have the students select two body parts. Tell the students they should explore all the ways these two parts can dance with each other, to move them close together and far apart, to move them like each other and different from each other. Try some of the following combinations:

- hand and foot
- knee and elbow
- fingers and toes
- head and hips
- shoulders and hips
- heels and toes
- hips and heels
- hips and toes
- elbow and heel
- knee and ear
- cheek and back

Glue Dancing

Tell the students a part of their body is glued to the floor. They should explore how they can dance with that part never moving. Parts that can be glued to the floor might include:

- one foot
- two feet
- one hand
- two hands
- two hands and one foot
- stomach

See also: 4.1 Parts on the Floor

1.3 Leading with a Part

Elf Ride

Bring out an imaginary box and tell the students the box has many tiny elves in it. Tell each student to take out an elf and place it on his or her elbow. The elbow should be bent in front of them. Tell the students to give their elf a tour of the room. Tell the students to move the elf to their other elbow and continue the tour. Tell them to move their elf to the bridge of their nose, to their hip, to their shoulder, wrist, knee, etc.

Later, tell the students to dance around the room while balancing their elf on various body parts.

Going Fishing

Have the students go to one end of the room. Tell the students you are going to pretend to throw out your line and catch them by the ear and say, " I'm reeling you in. I'm reeling you in. I'm reeling you in and I cut the line and you swim away." Repeat and catch them by their shoulder, their knee, and their toe. Have them chose a part and show you which part they were caught by.

Roller Coaster

Have students scatter around the room. Tell them their hands are the cars on the roller coaster track. Have students move around the room following their hands as the teacher describes the ride. Include moves such as:

- going up to the top
- blazing back down
- sharp turn one way
- a sharp turn the other way
- over some bumpy hills
- back up a big hill
- 2 large loops
- long slide home

1.4 Initiating with a Part

Making Circles

Lead the class in making circle motions with one finger. Tell the class to make the same motion with a finger on their other hand. Tell them to make that motion from their wrists; from their elbows; their shoulders; using the whole top part of their body; using their whole body; using the whole room!

Try a different initiating motion such as tapping one toe. Explore that motion with other body parts.

Theme 2

Awareness of **TIME**

Theme 2: Awareness of Time

2.1 Quick and Slow Movement

Fast Land/Slow Land

Divide a room in half and have half the class on one side and half on the other side. Tell the class that one side of the room is "Fastland" where everyone moves about very fast. The other side of the room is "Slowland" where everyone moves around very slow. Tell the class they should move around in their land for a while and then cross over into the other land for a while and then return to their land.

Big Bubble

Move around the room as if inside a large bubble.

Butterfly Hands

Flutter hands very quickly like butterflies and tell the students to show a butterfly dance.
Classical music that works well to support this activity;
"Flight of the Bumble Bee" by Nikolai Rimsky-Korsakov.

2.2 Clock Time

How Long Is a Minute?

Tell the class to move around the room for 30 seconds and to stop when they think 30 seconds is up. Tell them not to count seconds but to simply stop when it feels like 30 seconds. Try other durations.

I'll Count to 10

Have a group of students move to one end of the room. Tell them at the other end of the room is an imaginary wall. Tell them that you will count to 10 and you want them to arrive at the wall as you say the number 10. Don't be early…. don't be late. After they have reached the other end have the students turn around. Now they should arrive at the imaginary wall at the other end as you count to 15. Try counting to 20 or 5!

Variation: Have students select two spots in the room. Tell them to travel from one spot to the other in 10 counts. Try other numbers as they travel back and forth between the two spots.

Different Parts/Different Times

Have the students sit on the floor in a circle. The teacher should tap a beat on a drum at slow to medium speed. Have the students follow the directions while you continue tapping on the drum.

- stand up in 6 taps
- sit down in 3 taps
- raise both hands above your heads in 2 taps
- lower your arms in 1 tap

- bend your head forward in 10 taps
- lift head up again in 2 taps
- lift one leg in 5 taps
- put it down in one tap
- bend over to one side in 4 taps
- sit back up in 3 taps
- lift both legs in 7 taps
- drop both legs in 1 tap
- bring knees to chest in 2 taps
- put knees down in 8 taps

Being Bigger and Smaller

Have the class explore how small they can be. Ask them to get bigger and explore how big they can be. Now tell the class you want them to be as small as they can be and you will count to 8. They should get bigger as you count to 8 and be the biggest they can be when you get to 8. Do the same as they get smaller. Try different numbers as they get bigger and smaller.

See also: 3.1 Couple Dance
4.1 Elevator Ride
9.2 Balloon

Theme 3

Awareness of SPACE

Theme 3: Awareness of Space

3.1 Personal Space and General Space

Inside the Bubble

Pretend to hold a bottle of bubbles and a bubble wand and blow imaginary bubbles out into the classroom. Each student should let a bubble land on the palm of his or her hand. Each student should then take out an imaginary straw and place one end into the bubble and then blow the bubble up bigger and bigger. Tell students to step inside their bubble. Have students paint the inside of their bubble using each hand as a paintbrush. With this exercise the students are clearly defining their personal space. Now ask the students to move with their bubble somewhere else in the room…and then move back. In the future try having the students "get inside their bubble" before lining up at the door or going down the hallway.

Classical music that works well to support this activity:
- "The Fish" from Carnival of the Animals by Camille Saint-Saëns
- "Moonlight Sonata" 1st Movement, by Ludwig van Beethoven

Couple Dance

Students should work with a partner. One student moves in his/her personal space and the other moves around their partner using general space. The teacher could play a beat on a drum and tell the students to switch roles every 8 beats. Try switching roles with more and less beats.

3.2 Direct/Indirect Pathway (Straight/Twisted)

Here and There (straight)

Students should find a spot in the room and stand there. Have the students look for another spot in the room and then go there using as straight a pathway as possible without bumping into anyone else. They should then return to their original spot in the same manner.

Here and Indirectly There (twisted)

Students should find a spot in the room and stand there. Have the students look for another spot in the room and then go there using as twisted a pathway as possible without bumping into anyone else. They should then return to their original spot in the same manner.

We All Stand Up (straight)

Have the students stand up and slowly raise their hands above their heads. Now, slowly lower hands and sit down. This movement could be accompanied by playing a chromatic scale on an instrument. (Contrast with "We Raise Our Twisting Hands" below.)

We Raise Our Twisting Hands (twisted)

Tell the students they are to stand up slowly and raise their hands above their heads but have their hands follow a most twisted pathway. Now, slowly lower hands following a twisted pathway and sit down. Perhaps accompany this by playing a chromatic scale on an instrument (up some, down a bit, up some more, back a bit, etc...).

Crossing the Circle (straight)

Have students stand in a circle. Have them look directly across the circle to see who is there. Ask the students to go where that other person is as straight as possible without bumping into anyone. The circle should disappear and then re-emerge. Then students should return to where they came from.

Shape Gossip

Have students stand in a line facing the back of the person in front of them. (Form two or more lines if it is a large group.) The teacher should draw a shape on the back of the last person in line. That person then draws the shape they felt on the person in front of them. Continue until the first person in line feels the shape on his/her back. Have that first person draw the shape they felt on a blackboard or easel. Have the group compare this shape to the shape they felt on their back.

Finger Drawing

Prepare a set of cards with shapes drawn on them. Have the students arrange themselves in a circle. Give each student one of the cards and ask that student to use their finger to draw that shape in the space in front of them. Then pass their card to the next person in the circle. Continue until all students have had the chance to draw all of the shapes. Later, show one student one of the shapes and have that student draw that shape in space. Have the others guess what the shape is.

Walk My Walk

Have all of the students come to one end of the room. Have them watch the pathway that the teacher walks (perhaps a circle to start). After the teacher is finished with the pathway have the students walk one at a time, where the teacher walked. Try many different pathways. Later, have individual students create the pathway for the others to follow. Also try showing drawings of shapes and have them walk the shape or ask students to draw shapes they have traveled.

Walk This Way

Prepare a set of cards with shapes drawn on them. Show one student one of the shapes and have that student draw that shape in space by walking it in the room. Have the others guess what the shape is.

Home Decorating

Give each student an imaginary pot of paint. Ask the children to use their pointer finger and decorate their room with circles, spirals and figure eights. Make big and small shapes. Make the shapes near and far.

3.3 Inward Movement (Narrow)

The Shrinking Bubble

Have children get inside their imaginary bubbles (see 3.1). Tell them to use their hands as paintbrushes to paint the inside of the bubble as the bubble slowly gets smaller and smaller.

Cave of Spider Webs

Have students go to one end of the room. Have them travel to the other end of the room imagining they are in a cave with spider webs. Move across the room trying not to touch any of the spider webs that are all around.

Inner Tube Squeeze

Have students imagine they have an inner tube and the hole in the middle is not very big. They should push their arms through the hole and put it over their head (like putting on a sweater). Continue pushing the inner tube down the entire length of their body until they can remove their feet from it.

Subway Squeeze

Have students imagine they are on the subway and more and more people keep getting on until it is very full and all the people are tightly squeezed together. Tell them they have to get to the door to get off at the next stop so they will need to squeeze past all of the people to get to the door at the other end of the car.

Shrinking Room

Tell the students to dance around the room with the largest motions they can. At a given signal the room is now half the size and they can't make their motions as big anymore. Again the signal sounds and the room is smaller still. Continue until the room is very small.

3.4 Outward Movement (Wide)

Expanding Bubble

Have children get inside their imaginary bubbles (see 3.1). Tell them to use their hands as paintbrushes to paint the inside of the bubble as the bubble slowly gets larger and larger.

Balloon

Have students become as small as they can. Then tell them to slowly expand like a balloon being blown up; bigger and bigger. Tell the students you will slowly let the air out. Then blow the balloon up again. Finally the teacher may either say "pop" or "let go," meaning the balloon will fly around the room and then collapse.

Fireworks

Tell the students that their hands are fireworks. As you play occasional crashes on a cymbal have the students throw their hands up and out like fireworks exploring. Later, tell the students to dance around the room and occasionally use their whole bodies to represent the fireworks exploding.

Sewer Pipe

Have students go to one end of the room. Tell them we will pretend to walk through a sewer pipe. It is a very hot day and feels good to have our hand reach out and feel the cool walls. Be sure to walk with feet apart to avoid stepping in the stream that runs down the center.

Finding Your Way

Have students go to one end of the room and tell them to pretend they are in the dark and cannot see. Have them pretend to reach out to feel their way as they work their way to the other end of the room.

Growing Apart

Have students work in pairs. Have them dance together by either imitating one another or by doing something different. They should begin the dance very close to each other with small movements. As the dance continues tell them to use bigger and bigger movements and dance further and further away from each other.

3.5 Direction of Movement

Mass Move

Have all the students stand close together as a clump. Speak directions for the clump to shuffle; such as move toward the door, toward the front, toward the window, toward the floor, toward the ceiling, toward the back, toward me, toward the aquarium, etc. The challenge is for the clump to remain a clump!

Looking Up, Looking Down

Tell the students that in this dance they must either look up or down all the time. Tell the students to look up at the ceiling while gradually going down to the floor and standing back up. Ask them to continue looking at the ceiling while doing other motions such as:

- moving forward
- moving backward
- moving sideways
- stretching
- twisting
- wiggling
- shaking

Now ask the students to dance while looking down all the time. Do the same activities as before. Finally ask the students to do the dance once again while looking straight out. After, ask the students how it felt different doing the motions looking up or down as opposed to looking straight out. Children often look down while dancing. Looking up or down tends to restrict movement. Help them become aware that looking out allows their motions to be more full. Also try having the students do the previous motions while:

- choosing a spot and keeping their eyes fixed on the spot
- choosing another person and keeping their eyes on that person

Facing the Wall

Have students imagine that they have three faces; their real face, one on their chest and one on their belly. Have them direct all three faces to the same wall. Ask the students to dance with all three faces continually looking at the designated wall. Ask the students to do other motions while keeping their faces on the wall such as:

- travel sideways
- toward the wall
- away from the wall
- stretch
- jump
- sink
- float

Later, have the students keep their real face on one wall and their other two faces on a different wall while performing the previous motions.

Direction Dance

Create a string of prepositions and chant the sequence for a dance. Have all the students come to one end of the room. Have three or four at a time move across the room reflecting the words being chanted such as, "Over, under, around, out, in, in." Later, practice with a partner and perform the sequence for the class.

Variations:

"Go, go, go, go round shape (hold it) slow change to straight."

"Front, front, front, front, make a shape, away, away, away, together, together."

"Low, low, low, low, high, high, high."

"Straight, straight, straight, straight, around, around, around, around."

"Over, under, around, out, in, in."

Later, try reciting these sequences as the students travel from one end of the room to the other end of the room.

"Hands reach, they shake,
They pull you till you stop.
Skip and skip and skip and
Jump, jump, jump."

Or, with a partner:

"Front, front, front, front, (perform
    side by side with partner)
Make a shape;
Away, away, away. (away from partner)
Together, together."

3. 6 Distance of Movement

Measure the Distance

Have each student write their name on a small "sticky" paper and go to one end of the room with their paper. Place a piece of masking tape on the floor. Ask each student to go forward from the tape 20 feet and place their paper on the floor where they think 20 feet is. Bring out a measuring tape and measure to see who was the closest. Repeat with other distances.

Walk How Far...

Have the students find a place to stand in the room. Tell them to walk forward as far as it is from one end of their bed to the other. Have them walk how far it is from one end of their bicycle to the other. Have them walk how far it is from one end of their parent's car to the other. Walk how far it is from the TV to where you sit and watch; etc…

With These Two Parts I Show

Ask the students to select two parts of their body. Now, with those two parts show how big your favorite box of cereal is. Select two other parts. Show how big your favorite crayon is. Continue selecting two body parts and imagining the size of familiar objects.

Loud Is Big, Soft Is Small

Tell the students that when the drum is tapped softly they should take small steps around the room. When the drum is hit loudly they should take large steps around the room. Have the students move around the room as the drum is loud and soft, and gradually becomes louder and softer.

Theme 4

Awareness of LEVELS

Theme 4: Awareness of Levels

4.1 High/Middle/Low

Sit Down

Have everyone sit down on the floor. Ask each student to notice the shape of his or her arm. Ask all to stand but not to change the shape of their arm. Ask everyone to raise their arm as high as they can without changing the shape. Now lower the arm and sit back down on the floor and place your arm in exactly the same place it began.

Refrigerator Box

Tell the students to imagine a neighbor has just gotten a new refrigerator and put the box it came in outside. Let's make a clubhouse out of the box. Have all get inside. Have all paint the ceiling, paint the walls and paint the floor. Paint a door and a window. Paint a light on the ceiling.

Counting Shapes

Divide the class into two groups, the "performers" and the "audience." Ask the performers to dance showing their favorite movements and when they hear the tambourine they should freeze, ending in a shape that is either high or low. The audience should count how many are high and how many are low. After a few dances, switch roles. Later, divide the students into smaller groups and tell

them when they hear the tambourine their group should freeze with one of the following:

- more low than high
- equal numbers of low and high
- twice as many low as high
- more high than low
- twice as many high as low
- only two high, the rest low

Also try other contrasting shapes such as:

- wide and narrow
- round and straight

Also try combinations such as:

- high, low, wide and narrow

Group Shapes

Divide the class into small groups. Tell them to create three different group shapes that contain some high shapes and some low shapes. Tell the students they will have to decide how to transition from each group shape to the next, such as move fast to one and slow to another, or "jiggle" from shape to shape. Later, ask the students to create group shapes with the following:

- more low than high
- equal numbers of low and high
- twice as many low as high
- more high than low
- twice as many high as low
- only two high, the rest low

Elevator Ride

Tell the students to scatter around the room and squat down. Tell the students they are going to ride on an imaginary elevator in a building that has 10 floors. Start by riding the elevator all the way to the top while counting from 1 to 10. Then call out numbers and have the students find the appropriate level. Try this activity at different speeds. At first tell the students that the elevator is very slow. Then tell the students the elevator is fast, very fast, sort of slow, etc. Later, have the students work in pairs. While facing each other they should take turns calling out floors for their partner to go to.

Parts on the Floor

Tell students to have two body parts on the floor all the time and move from one place to another. Tell them to have 3 parts on the floor and move. Try other numbers.

Not My Level

Have students work in pairs and move around the room. One person is the leader and moves varying the level that he/she is moving. The partner must move with the leader but never at the same level. Sometimes the leader should change levels slowly and other times quickly.

Vertical Twister

Give directions to the class so they will be placing body parts at high, middle and low levels. For example, put a low body part at middle level and a high body part at low level or try two high parts at low level and one middle part at low level. Try various combinations.

Trio Statues

Working in groups of four, have one person be the sculptor and the other three be the statues. The sculptor must make a group shape out of the other three but one must be a high shape, one must be a middle shape and one must be a low shape. Repeat the activity until each has had a turn to be the sculptor.

See also: 3.1 Inside the Bubble
9.1 Distorted Mirrors

Theme 5

Awareness of WEIGHT

Theme 5: Awareness of Weight

5.1 Heavy/Light

Push the Refrigerator (heavy)

Tell the class to imagine they are standing next to the refrigerator. Something very special has fallen behind it (a quarter, a CD, a book). You only need to move the refrigerator over about one foot to be able to reach it. Ask students to press their whole body against the refrigerator and push as hard as they can. It does not move. Press harder. It moves a little. Press again and again. It moves a little more and a little more. One last push. Yes, now the object can be reached.

Building a Snowman (heavy)

Tell the students they are going to build a snowman. They begin with a small ball and roll it in the snow. As they roll, it becomes bigger and heavier. Push it until it is too big to push any more. Begin rolling a second ball. When the second ball is too big to move lift it up onto the first ball. Roll one final ball. When finished rolling place it on top of the snowman.

Classical music that works well to support this activity:

• "The Elephant" from Carnival of the Animals by Camille Saint-Saëns

See also: 8.2 Ball of Space

5.2 Strong/Gentle

Break the Balloon (strong)

Tell students to imagine they are each holding an inflated balloon under their arm with their arm wrapped around it. Inside one of the balloons is a coupon for a hot fudge ice cream sundae. Now they have to break the balloon by punching the balloon with their fist. Punch again and again; harder and harder. Finally place the balloon on the floor and stomp on it with one foot. It breaks! The coupon was in the teacher's balloon. Better luck next time!

Tap the Bubble (gentle)

The teacher should hold an imaginary bottle of bubbles and a bubble wand and then blow bubbles out to the class. Each student is to gently tap the bubble up into the air. They should continue tapping it to keep it afloat and gradually move the bubble to the other side of the room.

Eggshell Floor/Imaginary Drums

Tell the students to pretend the floor is made of eggs and that they have to dance on the eggs without breaking them. To do this they must move in a light, gentle and delicate way. Also tell them that there are small drums hanging in the air and that when they hear the tambourine they should stop walking on the eggs and make the loudest imaginary noise they can by hitting the imaginary drums as hard as they can. Switch back and forth between walking on eggs and hitting the imaginary drums each time the tambourine is tapped.

5.3 Tense/Relaxed

Trust Your Partner

Working in pairs, one person (A) lies on the floor while the other (B) sits next to them. B lifts A's arm. A should be totally relaxed and trust B. B moves A's arm up and down and around. Repeat with other arm. Repeat with one leg and then the other. Repeat with A's head. Reverse roles and repeat the entire routine.

Resist Your Partner

Working in pairs, one person (A) lies on the floor and the other (B) sits next to them. B attempts to lift A's arm. A should resist B. Repeat with other arm. Repeat with one leg and then the other. Repeat with A's head. Reverse roles and repeat the entire routine.

Theme 6

Awareness of
LOCOMOTION

Theme 6: Awareness of Locomotion

Walking, leaping, running, hopping, jumping, skipping, galloping, striding, sliding, crawling, rolling, tiptoe, stomping, etc…

Do As I Do

Ask students to walk around the room and notice the leader. When the leader stops, all should stop.

When the leader walks, all should walk. After stopping, the leader can choose other ways to travel around the room. Each time the students should move in the same manner as the leader. Invite other students to be the leader.

Move When I Stop

Ask the students to stand still while the leader walks around them. When the leader stops, all students should begin walking and continue until the leader begins walking and then they should all stop. Each time the leader begins moving he/she should try a different way to travel. Each time the leader stops the students should travel in the manner that the leader did.

Don't Move Like Me

Ask the students to stand still while the leader walks around the room. When the leader stops, all students should begin traveling in a manner different from the leader. When the leader begins moving again the students should stop. Each time the leader stops the students should move in a manner different from the leader. If the leader moved high, the others should move low. If the leader was quick, the others should be slow. Later, invite other students to be the leader.

Word Cards

Prepare a set of large cards with one action word written on each card. Spread the cards face up all around the room. Have each child find a card and stand by it. At a given signal have the students begin moving in the manner stated on their card. They should continue moving that way until they arrive at another card. They should then begin moving in this new way. Have the students continue traveling from card to card until they have tried all of the motions.

Skipping Dance

Tell the students that this is a good dance to find out all the things they can do while they are skipping. Tell them that no matter what happens they must keep skipping. Tell them you will call out things for them to do while they are skipping and they should not be tricked into stopping, jumping, walking or running. Call out directions such as:

- stretch
- twist
- skip backwards
- go in a circle
- etc…

Try this activity while students are traveling around performing other locomotor movements.

Theme 7

Awareness of FLOW

Theme 7: Awareness of Flow

7.1 Sudden/Sustained

Statues

Tell students that they should create a statue and freeze when you play the tambourine. While students are frozen tell them to remember the statue because they will make it again but now think of a different statue to turn into when the tambourine is played. Hit the tambourine. Tell the students each time the tambourine is played that they are to change to the other statue. Hit the tambourine for the statues to change two or three times.

While students are still frozen tell them to slowly change to the other statues as you gently shake the tambourine. Have the students slowly change back and forth between the two statues while being accompanied by the tambourine.

Now, tell the students to listen to the tambourine. If it is struck, they should quickly change to the other statue. If it is shook they should slowly change to the other statue. The teacher should vary stricking and shaking the tambourine.

Paint the Room

Divide the class into two groups. One group will paint the room by dabbing dots. The other will paint the room with long sustained gliding brush strokes. When the tambourine is hit the two groups should reverse roles. Switch back and forth.

Breathe and Flow

Have students focus on their breathing. With each inhale flow in a sustained motion into a shape. With each exhale flow in a sustained motion into another shape. Also try moving around the room. With each inhale or exhale take a step and flow in a sustained motion into a shape. Later, ask students to breathe slower or faster and reflect their breathing in their flowing from shape to shape.

See also: 9.1 Echo Motions and Shapes

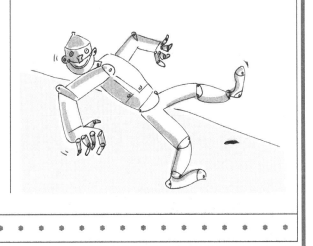

7.2 Sequential/Simultaneous

Wave

Have all students stand in a circle. The teacher serves as the leader. The teacher should slowly raises his/her arms and the students should mirror the teacher. The teacher should move his/her arms in various directions and students should try to move simultaneously with the teacher.

Now have the students all turn in the same direction and face the back of the person in front of them. Tell the students to only watch the person in front of them and move in the same manner as that person. Again, the teacher should serve as the leader and the students should imitate the teacher's moves. The movements will travel around the room like a wave. Later select individuals to serve as the leader.

Also, try passing other movements around the circle or even passing a face around the circle!

Who's the Leader?

Select one student to leave the room. While that student is gone, select another student to be the leader. Tell the class not to look directly at the leader but look directly across the circle and try to do whatever the leader does simultaneously. The leader should occasionally change motions. When the student is brought back into the room, he/she will stand in the middle of the circle and have three guesses as to whom the leader is. The leader should only change to new motions when the person in the center has his/her back to the leader.

Marionette

Have students stand tall with arms at their sides. Tell the students they are puppets and you have string attached to their head, to their shoulders, to their upper back, their middle back and their lower back. Tell them you will slowly lower the strings one at a time but none of them should fall down. First tell them you are holding the string for their head and are slowly lowering it until their chin rests on their chest. Next hold the string for their shoulders and slowly lower the shoulders. Do the same for the upper back string, the middle back string and the lower back string. After all the strings are lowered the students should be leaning over with their arms hanging down (successive movement down). Now, take each string and slowly pull that string back up. Start with the lower back string, then the middle back string, the upper back string, the shoulders and finally the head (successive movement up). All should be standing tall. Now tell the students that a giant pair of scissors has come and will cut those strings all at once. Clap your hands as the strings are cut (simultaneous).

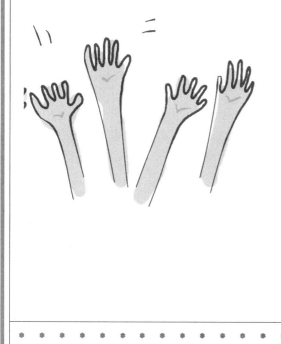

7.3 Bound/Free

Room of Jell-O

Divide the class into two groups with one group at each end of the room. Tell the group that last night, when no one was looking, someone came and filled the room with Jell-O. Slowly and with effort push and pull each body part through the Jell-O. Try to use different body parts to be the first part through the Jell-O then pull the other body parts through. Continue until all children have arrived at the other end of the room.

Classical music that works well to support this activity:

- "Air" from Orchestral Suite No. 3 in D by Johann Sebastian Bach
- Adagio by Albinoni
- "Largo" from Xerxes by George Fredrick Handel
- 2nd Movement, Oboe Concerto in D minor by Johann Sebastian Bach

Magic Gloves

Tell students you have a box filled with magic gloves. Walk around the room with the imaginary box and allow each student to reach in and pull out a pair of gloves. To enhance the fantasy ask students to describe their gloves to the class. Now, tell the students the gloves have started to make their fingers slowly start moving. Then the gloves are making the fingers move faster. The gloves are making their fingers wiggle quickly while their hands are being made to move up and down and all around. The more the students try to stop the gloves the faster and more erratic the gloves move. Suddenly, the gloves stop. Take them off and throw them back into the box. Whew!

Try a variation of this activity with magic slippers.

Rusty Tin Man

Tell the students they are made of tin and they have been left out in the rain and now they are rusty. It is very difficult to move. Have the students travel around the room.

See also: 1.1 Paper Plate Balancing

Theme 8

Awareness of SHAPE

Theme 8: Awareness of Shape

8.1 Becoming Shapes

Shape Cards

Prepare a set of cards with shapes drawn on them. Have the students arrange themselves in a circle. Give each student one of the cards and ask that student to make themselves look like that shape. Then pass their card to the next person in the circle. Continue until all students have had the chance to make all of the shapes. Later, show one student one of the shapes and have that student make his/her body into that shape. Have the others in the class guess what the shape is.

General Shapes

Ask students to move around the room and when they hear the tambourine they should freeze in a general shape such as a:
- comfortable shape
- sitting shape
- standing shape
- round shape
- straight shape
- low shape
- twisted shape

Object Shapes

Ask students to move around the room and when they hear the tambourine they should freeze in a specific shape such as a:
- letter
- toy
- breakfast food
- piece of furniture
- turtle
- skyscraper
- icicle

Ask the other students to guess the object.

Letter Shapes

Ask students to make a shape that looks like a letter that has only straight lines. Make a letter that has only curvy lines. Make a letter that has straight and curvy lines.

Later, ask the students to be the first letter of some thing. Then be that thing.

Spelling Dance

Have the students think of a word they like (and they can spell). It could be their favorite color, toy, food, place, person or their own name. Have them make their body look like the first letter of the word. Slowly and carefully change into the next letter of the word. Practice a few times changing between the first two letters. Gradually add the rest of the letters. Tell them if it should be a sudden change or a sustained change. Have them spell the whole word but travel in some way to some other place between each letter.

Pass the Space Ball

Have students sit in a circle. The teacher shows an imaginary ball of space and hands it to the next student in the circle. That student takes the ball and hands it to the next. Continue until the ball returns to the teacher. Next, tell the class, that after receiving the ball they can stretch the ball larger or press it in smaller. They should then hand the ball in its new size to the next person in the circle. Continue until the ball comes back to the teacher.

Later, the ball can change size and/or weight. Also, try passing the ball with other body parts such as feet or pass it with something flat or something heavy.

Space Ball Dance

Have students create their own imaginary ball of space. They should decide if the ball is small or large, heavy or light. Now, dance with the ball. Tell the students the size and weight can change as they are dancing with it. Other possibilities include dancing while:

- inside the ball
- standing on the ball
- throwing and catching the ball with your hands, or elbows, or knee or….
- leaping over the ball
- diving under the ball
- pushing the ball

Make My Shape

Divide the class in half. Half of the students should scatter around the room and make their bodies into interesting shapes and freeze. The rest of the students should dance around the statues. Gradually the dancing children should find a statue to stop by and imitate. Once the statue has been imitated the first statue can then begin dancing around the room, looking for some other statue to imitate.

Shape Chain

Have one student make a shape. The next student should make a complimentary shape and attach one part of his/her body to the first student's shape. One at a time each student should join the line. Once the last student has been added to the chain, the first student in the line can let go and join at the end.

See also: 9.2 Group Shapes

Theme 9

Awareness of OTHERS

Theme 9: Awareness of Others

9.1 Partners

Mirrors

Have students work in pairs. Tell the students that one of them is the mirror and the other is the leader. The leader should move slowly so the mirror can follow. Tell them to move so carefully that you cannot tell who is the mirror and who is the leader. Switch roles.

Traveling Mirror – Close and Far Apart

Have students work in pairs. Tell the students that one of them is the mirror and the other is the leader. While the mirror imitates the leader's movements both should move around the room, sometimes moving near each other and sometimes moving far apart from each other. Switch roles.

Distorted Mirrors

Have students work in pairs. Tell the students that one of them is a fun house mirror that distorts what is shown to it. The other is the leader. The leader will make movements and the distorted mirror will distort those movements. Switch roles. Also try having the mirror always reflect at a different level from the leader.

Gumby

Have students work in pairs. One student is a bendable figure and the other is the sculptor, shaping that person. The sculptor bends the other's arms, hands, legs, feet, body, head, etc. After the sculptor has finished, the sculptor should imitate the shape he/she has created and should hold that shape while the original bendable figure relaxes. Now the roles are reversed. The new sculptor reshapes the other person. Continue reversing roles. The teacher may suggest sculptural themes based on something the students are studying such as:

- geometric shapes
- amoebas
- robots
- animals
- historical figures

The teacher may also suggest various characteristics such as:

- angular
- jagged
- round
- bumpy
- tilting

Later, have students shape an imaginary person and make their body look like the shape they have created.

Tap and Flow

Have students work in pairs. One student is the sculptor and the other one is the statue. The sculptor makes gentle taps on various body parts of the statue. The statue responds to each tap with a short flow of that part. The sculptor continues tapping until he/she is pleased with the statue's shape. The sculptor should imitate the shape he/she has created and should hold that shape while the original statue relaxes. Reverse the roles. The new sculptor reshapes the other person. Continue reversing roles.

Magic Fingers

Have students work in pairs. One student is the magic sculptor and the other is the statue. The sculptor gestures with his/her fingers at various body parts but does not touch the statue. By making gestures like pushing and pulling, the sculptor molds the statue. The sculptor continues gesturing until he/she is pleased with the statue's shape. The sculptor should imitate the shape he/she has created and should hold that shape while the original statue relaxes. Reverse the roles. The new sculptor reshapes the other person. Continue reversing roles. Later try sculpting by making sounds near the body part you wish to move such as:

- clapping near partner's knee
- "shhh" sound near partner's belly
- stomping near partner's foot

Finger Follow

Have students work in pairs. One student is the leader and one is the follower. Have the leader hold out one finger and the student following should also hold out one finger and almost touch the leader's finger. The leader begins to slowly move his/her finger around and the follower follows with his/her finger. Gradually the leader begins to move the follower around the room, exploring pathways and levels. Switch roles. Try changing the distance between the fingers, leading from one foot away or from 10 feet away.

Complement a Shape

Have students work in pairs. One student begins by making a shape. The other student makes a shape that relates to the first shape either by imitating it or making a different shape that "fits." When the second student has made his/her shape he/she holds it while the first student relaxes, observes the second person's shape, and creates a new complementary shape. Continue taking turns making complementary shapes.

Later, have half of the pairs at one side of the room and the other half of the pairs at the other side of the room. Tell the students they are to make complementary shapes but each new shape should move closer to the other side of the room. Gradually the pair will end up at the other end of the room. Have both sides begin at the same time. Tell them, when they reach the other end to turn around and work their way back to their original side. Try staggering when the pairs depart. Have them count off. When the first pair is a short distance across the room the next pair should begin and so on. Have both sides begin at the same time. Try accompanying this activity with various pieces of recorded music.

Same and Different

One student is the leader and one is the follower. The leader makes a shape with his/her body and says either "same" or "different." The follower must observe the leader's shape and do as he/she is told. After a while, switch roles. Later, try the activity without the leader giving directions but by letting the follower choose to be the same or different. Perhaps have pairs perform their improvisation for the class.

Echo Motions and Shapes

Working in pairs, the leader performs a short motion that ends in a shape. The follower should echo the motion and end in the same shape. Later, explore motions that are sudden or sustained. Try having the follower perform the opposite flow (sudden or sustained) from the leader but end up in the same shape.

Movement Conversations

Have students work in pairs. Tell the students to have a conversation through movement. Alternate communicating to one another. Afterward ask the students to share what they were trying to communicate.

Connected to You

Have students work in pairs. Tell students to each select a part of their body and connect their chosen part to their partner's chosen part. Have students create a dance while remaining connected. Also, the teacher can call out two body parts and the students must figure out how to dance while connected to their partner.

See also:
  3.1 Couple Dance
  3.5 Growing Apart
  3.6 Direction Dance - Partners
  4.1 Not My Level
  5.3 Trust Your Partner

9.2 Groups

Mob Move

Have students stand very close to each other with their arms at their sides. Tell the group that no one is the leader. The group, as a whole should decide when it begins to move and stop and where it will move.

Group Shapes

Tell the students that in this game there is no leader and no one should talk or gesture to anyone else. Tell the students to make a circle. Tell the students to make a square, a triangle, a rectangle, an oval, a pentagon!

Balloons

Have the students in one large group or several smaller groups. Tell each group that they are a balloon. The teacher should count as the imaginary balloon is blown up. Have the circle expand as you count. Try the activity using different numbers. After the balloon is blown up the teacher can choose to pop the balloon or let the balloon go as it flies around the room as the air escapes. Tell the students to move appropriately when the balloon is popped or let go. The teacher may wish to use a real balloon to show what happens when it is let go.

Bigger and Smaller

Have students gather in small groups. Tell the groups they need to show how their group gets bigger while the teacher taps on a drum for 8 beats (gradually getting louder). Then the groups should get smaller while the teacher taps on a drum for 8 beats (gradually getting softer). Alternate between getting bigger and getting smaller.

Group Sculpture (complement a shape)

Have one student come to the center of the room and create a shape. Have another student come forward and make a shape that compliments the first shape. Continue having students add onto the shape one at a time until the group has created one large shape. Also, try asking students to attach to the shape in a prescribed way, perhaps with a thumb or knee or head. Once the group has made a sculpture tell them to change to a new sculpture when you strike the tambourine.

Later, try beginning with Complement a Shape (9.1) across the room and ending with a group sculpture. Complement this activity with recorded music and the students are ready for a performance!

Group Sculpture on the Move

Have students work in groups of four or five. Have one student begin by creating a shape and slowly moving around the room. Have another student make a shape that compliments the first shape and move with the first student. Continue having students add onto the shape one at a time until all in the group have created a group shape. Then, the first student moves away from the group sculpture and reattaches. Continue with students taking turns leaving the sculpture and reattaching.

Changing Group Sculpture

Divide the class into two groups. Half of the students should stand in the center of the room waiting to be sculpted and the other half are sculptors who should move around the group changing the shapes where they like; staying with one person as long as they like and then moving to another. Switch roles.

See also:
  1.1 Listen and Move
  1.1 Paper Plate Balancing
  3.6 Mass Move
  4.1 Counting Shapes
  4.1 Trio Statues
  4.1 Group Shapes
  7.2 Wave
  7.2 Who's the Leader?

Theme 10

STUDENT CREATED MOVEMENT

Theme 10: Student Created Movement

10:1 Representative Movement

Machine

Have students scatter around the room. Each student is a machine part and should create a stationary motion to represent that part. One student is selected to begin traveling. That student should travel in the way a machine part might move from one place to another. The traveling person should stop by a stationary person and begin to imitate that motion. The student who is being imitated may now start traveling. At first have just one person traveling at a time but later have several people traveling simultaneously.

Variation: The traveling person can tap a stationary part. Once the stationary part begins traveling the original traveler can sit down. This way every student will get a turn. Once everyone has had a turn try repeating the sequence having everybody going to the same person they did before. This time, when the traveling person selects a stationary person he/she imitates that stationary motion and the stationary person begins traveling. The sequence can be played with only one student moving at a time or the sequence can be initiated several times so several students are moving simultaneously. This activity can be accompanied with music. John Cage's "Third Construction" supports this activity.

Star Dance

Begin in a stooped position with both hands on the floor. This is a story of two stars.

As the sun went down the stars came up.
   Stand up very slowly and stretch hands above head.
One day one star started dancing.
   Slowly move one hand back and forth.
Then the other started dancing.
   Slowly move both hands randomly.
One star said, "follow me."
   Slowly move hands so one hand follows the other.
And the other star said, " follow me."
   Now the other hand leads.
One day they decided to dance through space.
   Slowly begin to travel around the room with arms slowly moving.
Sometimes they saw other stars and danced together.
   Without touching, one person places both hands near someone else's hands making an arch and then swaying their hands back and forth together. Other stars may see arches and fly under them.
Finally, the stars danced their way back home.
   Return to original positions.
And as the sun came up the stars went down.

Slowly return to a stooping position and place hands on the floor. Time the ending of the movement to end with the music.

Classical music that works well to support this activity:

- "Canon in D" by Pachelbel
- "Traditions of Christmas" from Mannheim Steamroller Christmas by Chip Davis

Space Ball Dance

Tell students they have an imaginary ball of space. Show how it looks to dance with it.

Halloween Dance

Have students dance the way their Halloween costume would.

Bubble Dance

Dance inside a bubble.

Ceiling Dance

Ask students to dance as if they could dance on the ceiling.

The Looberoos and the HopNPops (a story)

Divide the class into two groups. One group is the Looberoos and one group is the HopNPops. Have the students act out the following story as it is read aloud.

Once upon a time there were some Looberoos.

Once upon a time there were some HopNPops.

The Looberoos and the HopNPops lived in the same woods but they were not friends.

When Looberoos met HopNPops they put big frowns on their faces and stomped away.

Looberoos and HopNPops disagreed about everything.

Looberoos liked to be slow,

HopNPops preferred to be quick. (*Statues* 7.1)

Looberoos liked to be round,

HopNPops liked to be straight.

Looberoos liked to be low, HopNPops preferred to be high.

Looberoos were very proud of their feet.

HopNPops were vain about their hands. (*The Most Important Part* 1.2)

Looberoos liked to be the same as each other, HopNPops preferred to be different.

(Continue with your own list of opposites)

One day, the Looberoos had a very hard day. They had to jump, they had to stretch, they had to bend, they had to twist, they had to wiggle, they had to shake, they had to swim across the ocean and they had to bake a cake! At the end of the day they were so tired, they fell asleep standing up.

That same day, the HopNPops had a very hard day. They had to jump, they had to stretch, they had to bend, they had to twist, they had to wiggle, they had to shake, they had to fly across the ocean and they had to bake cookies! At the end of the day, they were so tired they fell asleep standing up.

Now, all the Looberoos and all the HopNPops were sleeping standing up. When you sleep standing up, you sometimes walk in your sleep, and when you walk in your sleep you sometimes dance in your sleep. So all the Looberoos and all the HopNPops walked to the same part of the woods and started dancing together. (*Partners* 9.1) And since they all slept with their eyes closed, they didn't know they were dancing with each other. And by the time they woke up, they were having such a good time that they decided to keep dancing together. And since they were going to dance together, they decided they ought to be friends. And now, every year they have the annual Looberoo and HopNPop parade.

10.2 Non-Representative Movement

Sometimes Free

Tell the students that you will call out words that tell them how to move. Students can choose whether they wish to move in personal space or in general space. Sometimes the words will direct them to move in a specific way such as:

- run curvy
- skip straight
- slide slowly

Other times say "free." Whenever the students hear "free" they should make up a way to move around the room that is different from the previous movement.

Opposite Dance

After the children have experienced moving and freezing, sudden and sustained changes, and low and high movements they can then be asked to create their own opposite dance in which they will decide when to stop and go, when to be high or low and when to change sudden and sustained. Ask the students to notice others around them and react to them by moving when someone is still, to relate to the shapes of other still people and find spaces to go over, under, around, between, etc. Remind the children that there will be no signals to tell them when to change but it will be up to them to sometimes go and sometimes stop. This activity works well in silence, with percussion instruments or with music. If performed with music ask students to dance in a way that compliments the style of the music.

Dancing with Form

As students create movement pieces discuss the possible forms that can organize a dance. Form such as:

AB
AABB
ABA
ABAB
ABBA
AABC
ABCD
ABACADA

A simple way for young children to be successful creating and remembering a sequence is to make the "A" section a shape, and the "B" section a movement. ABA is then a dance with a beginning, a middle and end (shape, move, shape).

Dance with the Music

This dance is pure movement improvisation. The children are free to move any way they feel. The only direction is to move the way the music makes you feel. Children may need some encouragement or suggestions at first and they may move very little or do one movement the whole time (running in circles is very popular). As they learn more possibilities for movement, their improvisations will become more and more interesting. You may want to find various types and styles of music to play in the background. Observe over time how the children learn to respond to the appropriate expressiveness of the music. You may want to remind the children of some movements that have been explored recently. You will probably want to provide some rules that address the following;

- safety: "No bumping into other children."
- variety: "Any movement except running."
- fun: "No dancing on the ceiling or windows."

Also include rules for what they can do, such as:

- "You may dance on the floor, in the air, on your toes, with a friend, backwards, with lots of stretching, etc. "
- "You may do any movement that we did today (or last time). "
- "You may do anything you have never done before. "

Sometimes do a long dance and tell the children this will be the longest dance they have ever done. These dances require patience on the part of the teacher but are valuable for children to have space to be totally creative.

Index